*Our Shared Breath*

First edition, February 2021
Copyright © 2021 Carolyn Chilton Casas

All rights reserved. This book or any portion thereof may not be reproduced or used in any manner whatsoever without the express written permission of the publisher except for the use of brief quotations in a book review.

**Published by Penciled In**
5319 Barrenda Avenue
Atascadero, CA 93422
penciledin.com

ISBN-13:		978-1-939502-42-1

Cover art
  *Mystic Realm* © by Blaire Kilbey:
  www.pixels.com/profiles/blaire-kilbey

Author photo
  by Robin Barnes
  www.robinbarnesphotography.com

Book and cover design
  by Benjamin Daniel Lawless

*Our Shared Breath*

by Carolyn Chilton Casas

# CONTENTS

## Where I Belong

- 2 — Where First Memories Were Formed
- 4 — Raspberries
- 5 — As a Child
- 6 — Where I Belonged
- 7 — I Come From…
- 9 — Running Away
- 10 — The Farmhouse That Held Me
- 11 — Things That Could Have Gone Wrong
- 13 — Shell Memories
- 15 — What My Father's Death Taught Me
- 16 — The Beating of Drums
- 18 — Connecting Between Worlds
- 20 — What Got Me to New York City
- 22 — Searching
- 24 — Calling All Angels
- 25 — *Ni Modo*
- 26 — Reiki for my Mother
- 27 — A Sixth Sense
- 28 — Letting it Fly
- 30 — The General
- 31 — Reflections at Day's End

## A Walk in my World

- 34 — Dear Agave
- 35 — My Companions
- 36 — The Most Beautiful Day
- 38 — The Pickers
- 39 — A Walk in my World
- 40 — New Year
- 41 — My Dear, Dear Friend
- 42 — Bring Me
- 43 — Humpback Gets a Taste of a Kayak
- 44 — Shells
- 45 — Thoughts on Life
- 46 — Detours
- 47 — Touched by an Angel
- 48 — Elephant Seals
- 49 — Unwelcome Serenade
- 50 — Ephemeral Youth
- 51 — Lately

## Mosaic in the Making

- 54 This is a photograph of me
- 55 Rhythms of Impermanence
- 56 Mosaic in the Making
- 57 Out with the Old
- 58 How I Feel About Turning Sixty
- 59 My Hands
- 60 Late Bloomer
- 61 At Last
- 62 Window Shopping for Words
- 63 Homage to my Single-Mindedness
- 64 Meaning of Christmas
- 65 Those Who Tend the Fire

## This I Believe

- 68 A Time my Own
- 69 My Voice
- 70 Gratitude
- 72 Go Easy
- 73 Imagine if
- 74 The Path to Choose
- 76 Motherhood
- 77 Dear one, whenever you are able
- 78 Questions to Myself
- 79 Thank you
- 80 This I Believe
- 81 Water
- 82 Reiki is
- 83 Equanimity
- 84 *Los Angeles*
- 85 Chosen
- 86 The Puzzle
- 87 Thanksgiving
- 88 Compassion
- 89 Things I Didn't Understand Were God
- 90 A New Day
- 91 That Ultimate Date
- 92 Another Approach
- 93 A Binding Thread
- 94 Graduation
- 95 When My Time Here

## *World Wound Down*

98 A Vision of Healing
99 We Are Told
100 Sheltered at Home
101 Animals During the Pandemic
102 A Friend
103 Land of the Free
104 The Significance of Corona
105 20/20 Vision
106 Giving Up Routines
107 Good News
108 Before the pandemic
109 Pandemic Pandemonium
111 Lockdown Lifted
112 Sentinels
113 Roadside Litter
114 A Continuance of Change
115 The Mask
116 These Days
117 *Una Sacudida*
118 The Grandmothers Answer
119 Practicing
120 Questions Google Can't Answer
121 World Upside Down
122 A Recipe
123 Because
124 Trespassing
126 Month Ten

I am grateful to the editors of the following publications where some of the poems first appeared:

*Ancient Paths*
*Central Coast Kind*
*Energy Magazine*
*Journey of the Heart: Women's Spiritual Poetry*
*Mujer Holística,* Mexico
*Odyssey,* South Africa
*Porter Gulch Review*
*Reiki News Magazine*
*ROC Metaphysical*
*SLO NightWriters* – Golden Quill Award
*Snapdragon: A Journal of Art and Healing*
*The Art of Healing,* Australia
*The Edge: Holistic Living*
*Your Daily Poem*

For my husband, Arguimiro, who was as surprised as I was
when, out of the blue, poems began dropping into my heart;
and for his patience when, in the middle of the night,
I get up to jot down words and lines.

For Allen and Elena, my children, who encouraged me to
follow my dreams and are the brightest lights in my life.

For my mother, Nancy, who has read more of what I have
written than any other person — without her insistence
that I put something tangible together, this book
would not have found form.

And for the loving practice of Reiki, the spark I believe started
it all.

When I cease to be on this earth's plane,
what to leave behind?

A legacy of love.

*Where I Belong*

## Where First Memories Were Formed

On sleepless nights
I fly to our family farm,
half a century gone by in time,
where first memories were formed.
Lifting up the gossamer thread,
I gently reel those days back to me.

It is morning; light streams
through the window in the second story
bedroom. I am alone and reach out my hand
between crib slats to the rays before calling out.

I am three, four, five, playing in gigantic lilac
bushes, creating make-believe rooms within
for a home of my own,
our cow dog Nicky at my side.

I collect eggs from the hen house,
play with the cats who live in the barn,
trail after my father as he stacks hay,
milks the cows and takes them to pasture.

My parents and I walk the path
through the woods to the lake,
past my mother's garden where the corn
grows tall and I help her pick carrots and beans.

I am six, seven, eight. The wooden porch door
slams thwack as I run through to the kitchen;
Mother bakes bread or pies,
on harvest days cooks for a crew,
or she sits at the table setting wet hair in curlers.

I hunt four-leaf clovers and watch as
grasshoppers bound from blade to blade
in front of the old icehouse. The dark,
treasure-filled attic calls to me, off-limits,
but I long to see the history hidden there.

My father and I are alone in an old rowboat;
I trail my hand through the water
as we glide by lily pads and cattails,
scenes I long to return to.

Burned down three decades past,
this farmhouse, the first place
to make its mark on me,
exists only in sleeping and waking dreams.

# Raspberries

The taste of a raspberry
takes me back,
every time.
I am a child, walking
through my grandfather's woods
toward the lake.

Tiny ruby gems
much smaller than
the store-bought ones
I savor now,
pinky-nail size, but oh
so lovely a treasure.

For just one more day
to be that small girl again
waking up in my slanted-ceiling
bedroom, with a view to the barn,
no cares, excited about
what the day will bring.

## As a Child

As a child I was most at home
outdoors, encircled by a wood of pines
laced with bluebells and lady slippers.

I climbed those trees, dug in the dirt
to find treasure buried by time,
left by an earlier people, delighted in

the open possibility of a rowboat
on a lake. I left a part of me
in that land of verdant dreams.

# Where I Belonged

Behind, in shafts of light on scattered hay
three city-dwelling younger cousins
wait, watching me in awe
to see if I will fly. Out the mouth
of a big red barn, I look dizzyingly down
to a mound of yellow far below.

The only child living on grandfather's farm,
I had been warned—the rope swing
out over the lake, water deeper than me;
the highway running past the house
where farmers drove at break-neck speeds;
the woods, not to go alone;
cavernous holes in the high haymow over
cement floors below.

Never had I possessed the courage to jump,
but this day, self-appointed tour guide
to the farm, I wanted to show my cousins
the world where I belonged.

Memory tells me I didn't do it; I chickened out.
Almost fifty years later, my cousin, Tim,
the spokesperson for his tribe, says
*You did it - you jumped that day!*

# I Come From…

— for my ancestors

I come from a farmhouse stoop at dusk,
cocooned in the comfort of grasshopper symphonies
and the fragrance of freshly mown hay.

From the mystery of a deep woods
where Chippewa Indians hunted
not so long ago.
My fingers held the proof,
the arrowheads they left for me to find,
just below the surface.

From pansies picked with my grandfather,
and peas shucked for my mother,
a grove of pine seedlings planted with my father,
a dog-wolf puppy bestowed by my grandmother.

From generations of westward pull—
Ireland, Switzerland, England,
Scotland, Wales, and France,
moving steadily to New York, New Jersey,
Ohio, Michigan, and Minnesota
to drop me in my dream California.

From hardworking pioneers,
descendants of persistent migration,
demonstrating by their histories
how to live with drive and determination—
Catholics, Mennonites, Methodists,
veterans of all the colossal wars fought
since our country commenced.

Thanks to you who came before me,
I come from a life like a diamond,
shining with multifaceted blessings,
a lodestar to love, a lifetime of being cherished.

# Running Away

Outside a clapboard cottage
surrounded by winter woods
on a bright, blue-cold Minnesota day
the girl lugs a barbie case
primed for escape,
the innocent plan to join her father,
weeks gone, working in a far-off town.

From a coal-heated living room,
mother and grandmother spy
on the bundled snowsuit child
as she slides down snow hills,
makeshift suitcase sled
filled with small shells, collected arrowheads,
and a few prized, much-read books.

When the cold winter wind is
no longer bearable,
warm, just-baked cookies entice her indoors,
to ease the ache of an absent father.

# The Farmhouse That Held Me

Abandoned, the firemen burned it down,
a handy practice maneuver, they said,
a necessity, conferred the relatives,
a liability for break-ins, the consensus.

Gone my childhood bedroom with sloped ceiling,
gone the attic and its longed-for treasures,
no more the kitchen where Mom made pies,
or the stoop, my place of peace at sundown.

Farmhouse from another century, generations back,
abides in photographs and memory:
my grandfather sitting in a lawn chair outside
while I played,
my mother's garden aplenty with food to be canned,
breakfasts of fresh eggs I gathered,
my dad stepping out the back door to care for the cows.

The barn still stands where I dunked the kittens
to bathe them, one by one,
in the icy milk tub; the only time
in my memory I made my father mad.

# Things That Could Have Gone Wrong

Most of us have a list
of close calls, those dreaded events
that easily might have materialized,
but mercifully did not.

My babies were born early,
one more than two months
before his time, both, thank heavens,
with no lasting conditions.

One time our toddler
opened a bottle of vitamins
containing iron; we rushed her to the hospital
to have her stomach pumped.

On a trip to Costa Rica,
our ten-year-old son was pulled
far from shore on strong currents;
a young man on the beach rescued him.

When our daughter
was just starting to drive,
and made a left turn
in front of a two-ton truck,
her car was destroyed, while she
walked away untouched.

There was a week I waited anxiously
for the results from a lump in my breast,
and later, held my breath
for favorable news
regarding my husband's tests,
which led to his treatment being suspended.

How often in the course of living
do we open ourselves unknowingly
to danger, yet survive?
Surely, angels with flawless timing
lift us away from calamity.

## Shell Memories

    *— for Mike*

I have always loved shells,
even as a child living on a farm
in Minnesota, where the only shells
were in my favorite picture book,
or the thin razor clams and tiny white
snails in my grandfather's lake.

Today, I walk our beach from Pismo
to Oceano with my husband,
telling myself, *You can look
but do not take any home!*

There, baskets and jars of all sizes and shapes
grace rooms, scooped up
lovingly on countless countries' shores,
decades of desire for their beauty fulfilled.

I remember another day, walking on Morro Strand
with my brother after a storm, sand dollars
floating in on the tide, glistening in multitudes,
covering the shoreline for miles.

It was before Christmas and I was enthusiastic
about making these perfect disks into ornaments
for gifts, nature's creation stamped by the cosmos
with a poinsettia and filled with tiny white doves.

He complained, grudgingly letting me
fill his pockets and his hands
for the long walk back to the car.
But he smiled as he grumbled,
and I could see this was a story
he would tell his children someday.

# What My Father's Death Taught Me

— for my father

*Such tragedy! how it takes death
to put everything in its right place,
how it takes death to perfect a life.*
            Perie Longo, "While Watching A Video
            of the Dalai Lama"

Eight years ago today,
my father took his last breath
in his TV easy chair,
yards from where I stood
chopping fruit for
my daughter's sixteenth birthday.

The hurt, more fierce
than any I had yet felt
sent me spiraling,
searching, and unfolding
almost in an instant.

In time, the only rational response
I could grasp was
to open my inner being
for all to see;
always, or whenever possible,
to exist vulnerably—
the sole means to heal
the sharpest sorrows
and to live a life of truth.

# The Beating of Drums

At the *pousada pequena* in a tropic beach town,
fatigued from too many hours of travel,
we were concerned when asked to leave
our room key hanging on the reception wall.

We had read State Department warnings
for tourists traveling to this area,
heard rumors to be careful, cautionary tales
about things being stolen.

A teacher at the school told me
her husband, an international pilot,
never left his hotel room in Rio
for safety reasons.  She hinted
Brazil was not the best choice for children,
hence, I was on high alert,
and somewhat alarmed about the key idea.

In the Sao Paulo airport, we had just met a family;
their son, fifteen, an exchange student who
stayed with us earlier in the year, and now
we were here to see the place he called home.

Our son had just turned eleven.
Having been given only a double bed
and a small cot for our daughter,
the family offered to let him stay,
the boys happy with this plan,
having shared a bunk bed months ago
and become friends.

Leaving our sons to catch up, we walked to dinner.
Like in many places with warmer climates,
the evening meal is eaten late;
at midnight, we strolled slowly back,
amazed to be suddenly in a place so foreign to us,
enjoying the fragrance of angel's trumpet,
a night-blooming flower.

Upon reaching their beach house,
we bid *boa noite* to our new friends
and continued down the dirt path to the inn.
The dad came running after us to say
their son had fallen asleep and ours was gone.
In his hand, a handwritten note, which read—

> *I couldn't sleep because of the drums.*
> *Outside, I yelled at them to stop.*
> *They didn't, so I am going to our hotel.*

We ran toward the Pousada Canto do Camburi
many dark streets away;
where we found no key on the wall,
took the steps two at a time
to the second story, and hurriedly
pushed open the door to find
our boy sound asleep on the tiny bed.

The next morning the Brazilian family
explained to our son—
the loud noises he had heard weren't drums
but the *ba, boom, ba, boom* of big frogs,
living in the jungle growth behind their home.

# Connecting Between Worlds

Driving through straw-colored hills of Andalusia
in our tiny rental car, and still missing
my father gone more than a year,
we have just completed the second leg
of our expedition from Seville to Lisbon.
My son and I plan to stay in small towns
along the way, a trip carefully arranged
for his summer break from college.

I am thrilled to have this time with my boy
as he begins his own journey toward manhood.
I yearn to share the stories with my father—
this wild adventure,
our first time in Spain and Portugal,
my son at twenty-one relieving me of the keys
in the Seville city center, saying, *I've got this, Mom.*
It is what I miss the most—talks with my father,
after dinner, over a cribbage game,
nearly every day of the sixteen years he lived with us.

In Arcos de la Frontera, we are gifted a corner room
in a quaint *parador* looking out over a deep canyon,
with birds soaring at our level.
On the balcony, wind whipping my hair,
my father's presence is strong.
I attempt to connect, asking if he is proud
that I have come so far out of my comfort zone
on this escapade with the grandson he very much loved.

At daybreak, creaking open wooden shutters
to a magnificent dawn over the canyon,
I turn on my phone to see the time.
There, a text from my brother reads,
*Dad is proud of you.*
I text back desperately, *What, how do you know?*

Not able to wait, I call, and he describes
the vivid dream he had hours after my attempted
communication, relating that it felt so real;
in his voice I hear how he has been touched.

*I ran to hug him, Carolyn;*
*it felt like dad, smelled like him.*
*The first thing he said to me was*
*I am so proud of your sister!*

# What Got Me to New York City

Each morning after breakfast, I start out
on a fast-paced stride toward a new Manhattan
neighborhood—Greenwich Village, Gramercy,
Chelsea, SoHo, Hell's Kitchen, Central Park,
logging six, eight, even ten miles
by afternoon's return to our Mid-town hotel.

On my hurriedly-jotted-down morning lists—
art and history museums, the Public Library,
Strand Book Store, Times Square, Central Park,
Fifth Avenue, cafes, and other urban landmarks.
I hike the High Line beside tall buildings
and take my first ride alone on a subway.

I had never desired to see New York City,
my life spent living in small towns.
A metropolis is not my idea of a vacation;
if I'm honest, they scare me.

What am I doing here?
The short answer: My daughter.
It is a covenant our children make, right?
Before leaving heaven and being born,
they must consent to help us become
more bendable, to stretch us as parents.

Somehow, after graduation we had agreed
to her plan—move all the way across the country
where she has found an internship. But there are
no friends here and the room she has rented
falls through. How did I allow this to happen?

But here I am, meeting her each evening
after work to explore more sections of the city,
helping her learn what she needs to survive.
Our last day together, we transfer
three, fifty-pound bags to a short-term rental,
practice her two-mile route to work,
study the subway entrances and exits
for dark evenings and cold weather.

Then, I leave her standing outside a building
on a street in Chinatown, alone,
to make her own way in the Big Apple,
my head reeling and my heart breaking,

as the taxi rushes me away to the airport
with my parenting agonies, and my daughter
starts off toward her happy ending,
four years later—a wonderful job, friends,
and a continuing love for the city she chose as home.

# Searching

My daughter is searching.
    *How do I reach a state of allowing?*
she asks one morning.

    *You believe everything*
    *happens for a reason, right, Mom?*
    *How can I find that faith?*

I am driving,
en route to an appointment;
the Bluetooth in my car is not clear.
She walks the streets of New York
on a break from work,
horns blaring in the background.
She wants an answer now.

I strain to hear her
urgent questions.
How to reply to this dear
daughter of mine so far away?
I struggle, searching for words
to convey what I believe.

    *Life experience has taught me*
    *that from the challenging times*
    *I grow the most.*
    *There has been a silver lining*
    *to each difficulty.*
    *Faith comes from this.*

*Allowing evolves from times
in silence, asking the Divine for guidance
then having patience to wait,
but also, being ever vigilant
for the answer.*

Though the connection is not strong
she hears me,
and I feel her take a deep breath
as she disconnects the call.

# Calling All Angels

An album holds photos of our toddler son
having fun with other children
in a small Mexican village,
dipping his toes into a frigid North Sea,
and on the back of my bicycle
in a countryside dotted with windmills.

As he grew, we saw more parts
of our spectacular world together,
push-pins spreading across
the map tacked up in his room.

So, I shouldn't have been surprised
twenty years later to be sitting
in an airport waiting to say goodbye,
he moving to a country six thousand
miles away, chosen at a spin of the globe,
where he knew no one, no job in sight
or place to live, not even speaking the language.

Having checked in a suitcase large enough
to stay for eternity,
the enormity of the decision he had set in motion
started to soak in and I felt his courage
begin to crumble.

When he went to the restroom
before boarding the flight, I silently
prayed to his guardian angels.
At that instant, the song
*Calling All Angels* began to play
on the airport speakers,
and I knew he would be okay.

# *Ni Modo*

— for Arguimiro

My husband is good
at accepting life as it comes.
He didn't even cry when his parents died,
whereas I weep for every loss.

His favorite expression
in response to life's tough times
is *ni modo*—a way of saying
oh well, it was not meant to be,
when he understands a situation
cannot be changed.

I admire his capacity to accept.
I would like to be more like that.
I imagine it is less painful
to welcome life that way.

# Reiki for my Mother

Wishing to unwind her life,
unfurl her troubles and fears,
she lies down on a warm spring afternoon,
semi-sleeping,
hand resting on her beloved black cat.

Seated by her side, my hands radiate
warmth above the part of her where I was formed;
a conduit connected us then,
her body offering the nourishment
needed for my unfolding.

Now, I seek to be the vessel
that conducts a flow of sustenance to her.

# A Sixth Sense

— for Catalina

Are we lulled by a perpetual parade
of days together?
Is a person's presence
more fully appreciated by their absence?

I try so hard to stay awake,
not to fall into the deep slumber
of forgetting, to remember
the impermanence of everything.

If only I had a sixth sense
to know when one I love will die,
then, maybe, I could ease
the dragon's weight upon my chest,
regretful and sad,
desiring to live another day from the past,
insisting things I might have done—
    those wishes not granted
    by the sorcerer of time.

# Letting it Fly

*If you love something, let it fly; if it comes back to you,*
*it is yours for now, if it doesn't it never was.*
             My grandmother Jeanette

I've never wanted to be that person
who keeps love locked up in a cage,
even though the risk is great
when you let life flow free,
that its coming back to you
might not be a part of the cosmic plan.

What I'm getting at are the daily
lessons of accepting change.
I cheered my children on
as they flew to far-off coasts and continents.
But now I cannot imagine this home
without my cat; for sixteen years
we have shared our daily lives:

>good morning meows
>as he comes in from his man cave;
>coffee together in bed while
>reading and writing poems,
>he on top of the purple pillow,
>paw resting on my arm
>or placed lovingly over my heart;
>sitting on my lap for Zoom classes;
>chatting while gardening,
>then before sunset, his bell and snack
>call him in to safety.

Yesterday he didn't come when I called.
I rang the bell and searched the hills, the brush,
even knocked on neighbors' doors.
As the sun went down, I turned on all the lights
and went to my chair to pray.

Hours after nightfall, he appeared
out of nowhere, meowing under my window—
proof in the power of love and letting go.

# The General

— for my mother

My mother is a force of nature,
her dream through sickness
and hospital stays
to bask in the big trees;
we made it come true,
curve by twisting mountain curve.

Her desire to visit the General—
with sticks she weaves and wobbles,
steadily striding onward,
one of us on each side,
toward the tallest tree.

A white-haired couple ambles down,
hand in hand, encouraging,
*You have almost arrived.*
They understand ambitions,
having travelled from Missouri
on motorcycle, solely to see the Sequoias.

Images captured from open windows:
flowing water vistas, icy peaks,
trunks and branches reaching
to the heavens; she is content.

All days are numbered,
many or few we cannot know.
*When I leave,* she announces,
*I'll fly over this place of God.*

# Reflections at Day's End

When I slip between the covers at day's end
or reflect in the quiet of first light,
a joy of gratefulness begins to flow
for a bounty of many blessings.

Family—hearts of my heart;
friends—bright spots of togetherness;
the land and wildlife—embraced and nurtured;
our home—where for years I have loved jubilantly,
and been loved.

All, I understand, is mine for a season,
will someday be the jewels of others.

*I shall vanish and be no more,*
*But the land over which I now roam*
*Shall remain*
*And change not.*
    Omaha Tribe, Hethu'shka Society

*A Walk in my World*

# Dear Agave

Through seasons and cycles
I observe your sturdy beauty
along our patio wall.

On summer days I sit with you,
lifting wind-blown twigs
from your concentric spirals.
On cold days
from windows I admire
your stoic strength.

Sensitive to September's searing sun
and winter's burning frost
parts of you perish,
tips of your leathery smoothness
turn brown, fold over;
under-leaves wither and fall.

But I have also witnessed the
wondrous marvel of spring
with its bounty of moisture and warmth
help you to birth new parts of yourself
that push out from your center,
perfect twisting curvy-coned babies
bursting out into our world.

## My Companions

A doe balances on hind quarters,
batting plums out of our tree
to let fall to her babies below.

Picking apricots in the orchard, I delight
in pogo-stick-legged young fawns
bounding through the field.

Day by day they find more valor;
venturing close to peek in.
Entire extended families have made
a lunch line through plantings
above the retaining wall, munching
what has been carefully tended, but I don't care.

When hares with extra-long ears hear me;
they freeze, thinking remaining motionless
is a cloak of invisibility. I assure them they are safe.

Hawks fly directly overhead, curious to see
what kind of being I am.
I love the sound of their heavenly cries
and the sight of their wing-spread bodies.
Owls screech after dark and again long before first light,
waking me. I welcome their wildness.

A vibrating whir of hummingbirds
is heard from every open window
and the jays tail obnoxiously after the cat
chastising him for who he is.
Squirrels make ruckus in the top of a pine;
lizards scuttle left and right as I walk down the path.

My magnificent friends move me to awe.

# The Most Beautiful Day

— for my volleyball friends

Carrying an old backpack from my daughter's
early school days, filled with water, hat, lip balm,
almonds, sunscreen, and lines, I bounce my weathered ball,
a Mother's Day gift from long ago, hand to air.

Down fifty steps to our perfect slice of paradise,
the aromas invade my senses,
urge me to appreciate again
the ocean fragrance which I could not live without—
sun, sand, salt, clouds, hills, bay.
A sigh releases as bare feet touch golden powder.

My friends await, burying stakes to form
our rectangle of revelry.  Thank you, Source,
for this devotion of mine, a spiritual practice,
no different than any other.

Oh, the striving for a perfect pass, a dig,
a tomahawk, a set placed close to net,
a spike in far corner, a dink, a lob touching line,
a cobra, arm extended to arc the ball,
a dive saving sphere from striking sand.
The pleasure of placing arms flawlessly,
seeing target only from edge of eye,
that agility I relive just before sleep.

*This is the most beautiful day!* They chuckle,
knowing I say this every time we play.

We continue after a crimson sun
sets behind alabaster clouds, the ball
no longer clearly discerned in the darkening sky.
It sprinkles as I walk to my car,
up the fifty steep steps,
legs weary, soul content,
on this jewel of a balmy evening.

# The Pickers

The squirrels have not yet found
the figs. They stole every single apricot
on the newly planted tree in days,
even though the roots are fortressed
to keep gophers out, the branches
fenced to protect from foraging deer.
Then the hellions pilfered half the plums;
I'd see them scurrying up the trunk,
running down with purple, ripe ones
in their overstretched mouths.

When they had eaten all the orchard's
harvest (the figs were not yet ripe),
the squirrels made do with their last resort—
the orange tree near the house.
I laughed to see one push a globe
up the hill toward her underground den,
maneuvering it with nose and neck,
only to have the sphere roll back down,
her darting after, to start all over again—
a modern-day furry Sisyphus.

Mostly I have given up and buy my fruit
at the farm stand around the corner.
But figs are my favorite;
I've rescued five so far.
Maybe the squirrels missed them,
don't like the taste, or they feel remorse.
Returning up the road from a walk, I spy
a squirrel scout peeking down the driveway;
our eyes meet, then he takes off,
sprinting full speed to warn his brethren,

*Here she comes, down the holes!*

# A Walk in my World

Down our narrow lane, turn right.
One more Indian summer day,
even this late in November.
A redheaded woodpecker beckons,
pecking away at a topless tree.

Almost at hill's crest, a young girl,
her mother, and small brother stock
their farm stand. The century-old clapboard
sits off to the side, reminding me of the house
where I lived at her age. We wave.
She's barefoot, minding her brother
like I would have been, marooned
on our wooded parcel, eager to see someone new.

In the '40s my father bought our house
by silent bid, five hundred twenty-five dollars
for the doctor's old residence on the White Earth Reservation.
He dug out a full basement on eighty acres
given to him by his father, then moved his proud
acquisition the short distance by hay wagon.

As I walk back down the hill, a red-tailed hawk
floats by; I call up and she circles overhead
in a spiral of recognition. A deer watches
as I pass by the neighbor's back fence,
undecided whether to bolt. I reassure him.
I think he knows my voice,
he a daily visitor to our home.

# New Year

Evening on the eve of a new year,
steeping in a warm bath of lavender
with a view to a rounded moon rising
between soaring eucalyptus trees
and smoke signal clouds,
diamonds at their edges.

A luminous orb, rivers of rays
stream out from the source,
lighting up the night sky.

The rabbit with his long ears,
read about in a long-ago *leyenda*,
guards our home from his radiant perch.

Remembering another New Year's Eve,
on a Brazilian beach, dressed in white,
wading in shallow ocean water—
seven waves to jump, a wish made for each.

# My Dear, Dear Friend

— for Chela

Perched atop a majestic mountain of sand,
scanning west to coastal waters,
we gaze down the steep decline
and my trepidation escalates.
Sensing my fear, she grabs me by the hand;
silently we descend running, swiftly though
each foothold slips and sinks deep below the surface.

Those midday jaunts no more, she
no longer accessible to hold my hand in life
like was her custom in the face of my fears.
Gone the guide, the mentor and caring healer
for countless needs of body and spirit.

I drive slowly by her house
on a common street through town,
picturing her husband remarried now,
and their children off starting new lives.
Slightly under the patina, our past conversations,
her sisterly presence an absence yearned for,
my dear, dear friend, mourned and missed
in manners too immense to describe.

# Bring Me

Bring me your sadness,
your worry,
your pain.

Together let us undam
a river of energy,
white and violet waters rushing
over the boulders
of your discomfort,

washing some stones
out to sea,
eroding others
to a smooth sheen,
rounded, more gentle to bear.

# Humpback Gets a Taste of a Kayak

My nephew texts from Idaho to ask
if I've heard what happened in Avila,
a bay close to our home.

Online, I watch the video, astounded
as a yellow kayak with two women inside
slides completely into the mouth
of a humpback whale.

They must have had a bird's-eye view
of its pink palate, the jaw's baleen
a curtain between fiction and reality.

For those minutes they were engulfed
within a giant, what were they thinking,
*It all ends here?*

Like Jonah, they were spat out,
only much sooner
than in the Bible story.

They can laugh about their close call now—
one joking about how lucky they were
to lose only their keys, not their lives,
the other making light that once on shore,
shaking her shirt, fish came tumbling out.

# Shells

From earliest memories I was drawn
to them, white spiraled snail babies
the size of a quarter or a dime,
found in the lake on the farm.

The razor-thin clams
didn't call to me as much,
but I liked to line them up at shore's edge,
to check their progress the next day.

Shells are coded into my DNA,
a message possibly from another lifetime,
personal gifts from the sea,
remembrances of places travelled far and wide.
Like a pirate digging up treasured loot,
always feeling I have found gold.

Their sea-smoothed softness,
beauty of design and hue,
my eyes can spot them
from a distance down the beach.
After more than fifty years of seeking,
I have mastered the seashell stoop.

Through the decades,
my affection for shells remains stable.
Shells—in bowls, on windowsills,
stowed in sweatshirt pockets,
a thread of continuity connecting me to the child,
girl, and young woman I was before.

# Thoughts on Life

Morning in the garden, my fingers combing
earth, when a screech grabs my attention,
out of the corner of my eye, our cat,
with a bunny squirming in his jaws.

I run after him, reprimanding,
*Let the bunny go!*
Gophers I can tolerate,
but bunnies no.

At night before sleep
an echo fills the room,
close coyote yowls, but by then
the cat is safe indoors.

Bearable now my memory of bunny,
instead of my beloved cat,
fickle, cutting in on God's dominion—
deciding who should stay and who may go.

# Detours

I never stop being amazed at
the suddenness of changes
we are pressed
to wrap our heads around.

Like the day my infant daughter
stopped nursing because she had a cold
and how she never came back to it again;
that first morning I dropped my son off
at preschool, his reaching out,
pleading for me to take him home;
or the heaviness around my heart as
my daughter took off in a car alone
with her new driver's license.

These are common detours in life.
We are made to yield to even bigger potholes—
wars, injustices, poverty, accidents,
illnesses, and death.
We fight against the rerouting of our lives
while at the same time knowing
we exist in a world where
anything can happen and often does.

# Touched by an Angel

— for Debbie

At first touch, a sigh releases;
she knows the spots that are stuck
and with long strokes starts to
unknot muscles along the spine
and down the legs from my hip.

My mind and then my body begin
to float away; dreamlike,
I bring them back again and again,
not willing to let this sense of heaven
slip away from consciousness.

Oh, the ecstasy of longer ligaments,
feet and hands kneaded with warm oil,
a body that gets untangled, revisits youth.
With deft fingers she creates more space
for life to enter in all its many forms.

# Elephant Seals

Oh, the body-surfing elephants
we saw down in the cove,
a-floating and a-bobbing
like buoys lost their moor.

They ride on playful waves
and hump up on the beach,
they bask in soothing rays,
flip sand onto their lumps.

Oh, the body surfing elephants
purr deep inside their throats,
I love to hear the chants they make,
to watch them bob and float.

# Unwelcome Serenade

Who would have known
one lone cricket
could make such noise.
Venturing into our living room
on an odyssey to a foreign land,
my husband tries to grab the intruder,
but he hops under the heavy Mexican bookcase.

When I attempt to sleep,
he sets up a serenade
by the bedroom door.

At two a.m., like an obnoxious tourist
leaving the bars, he sings drunkenly
through the corridors.

I dream of revoking his visa,
sending him back to his birthplace,
make devious plans for his deportation,
but the black bug evades us once more.

*Well, you always say you love*
*listening to the sound they make.*
    *I used to, but tonight I've changed my mind.*

# Ephemeral Youth

Warm Indian summer evening
   in Avila.  My husband and I sit,
      up on the cliff, car windows open,
         looking out over persimmon
           skies, eating child scoop
              ice cream cones.

A young man runs down the beach
   and does repeated handstands
      at water's edge;
         a young woman in bikini
           takes selfies as waves spill
              over her.

I wish to reach down
   and tell them
      *Good for you!*
         Enjoy your youth-filled
           puppy bodies.  They are
              ephemeral.  As is all.

# Lately

Lately, I have wondered if
    we are starting down a path
    towards a time
    when I will be alone.

Then I understand
    we set off on that course
    the minute I met you.

In the end
    we are meant to be alone.
    I will have to find the courage.

In a dream, we are sitting together
    in a church. You get up to leave
    without even a glance in my direction.
    I tap you on the shoulder,
    a reminder to come back for me.

*Mosaic in the Making*

# This is a photograph of me

See how fervently I try
to keep my world safe.

See how badly I want
a smooth, wakeless life.

I'm not a friend of change
although I would like to be.

# Rhythms of Impermanence

When life changes on a dime
and I am left with wounds from a rose
held too tightly, I must give myself
permission to skinny dip in the unknown.

When life once more transforms itself,
I must dance circles around the wild fire
of my future, while drums beat out
the rhythms of impermanence.

When life again shifts and alters,
as it is known to do, I must remember
that in this game of existence, to hold
love in your heart can be the winning card.

# Mosaic in the Making

It begins with the drawing of a vision,
    the design a yearning to discover the sacred,
    to express what is held inside.
Inspiration arrives with an alchemy of colors—
    I long for ocean celadon,
    shimmery silver of angels' wings,
verdant green of Amazon jungles,
    persimmon and magenta of day's end,
    ruby for living from an open heart.
Life is a mosaic in the making.

The moment comes to gently set
    the many tiny pieces of glass.
    One by one—the angles, curves,
and straight edges shape an intention,
    nudging the imagination to fly skyward
    in a labyrinth of discovery.
My mosaic is yet unfinished; that's how it is meant to be.
    Every masterpiece desires sufficient time
    for its becoming,
deliberately created, one dream at a time.

# Out with the Old

My car is ten years old.
*Too many miles; buy a new one,*
says my husband.
The carpet is worn;
one room has an unpleasant odor
where rain seeped in.
Verizon pronounces my cell phone
will no longer be serviced—
dated technology, the newest
version goes for a grand.
My son offers, *Join the modern world.*

The computer, where I write,
is ancient. The garden umbrella is dotted
with moss. Mesquite chairs
have scored the wood flooring.
Our dining table is marked by many meals.
Green grows on the stucco wall.
The washer smells and the refrigerator is loud.
A leather chair has been punctured
by roving claws. The stereo system is extinct.
Paint is peeling off the patio bench;
the cushions are faded. The beds all sag.
Everything demands replacing.

But I like them *all.*
I chose them with care
when I was also newer. I detest
discarding what is still of use;
it makes me weary to consider.
Can't we just be allowed to grow old together?

# How I Feel About Turning Sixty

Sixty does sound oodles older
than fifty-nine, more like
a senior citizen
than a mid-life *You Rock This*,
closer to a crone,
or should I say wise woman
or elder, maybe I could try those mantles
on for size.

Thankful to be where I am—
hardy of mind, body, and soul,
to have come out the other side
of a few difficult times.

Thankful to have had the journey
of being a mother—so much joy
from that realm, and a wife
who has been greatly cherished.

Thankful for the lessons
I've learned along the way.
For sure I'd never swap them
for a chance to be twenty again.

## My Hands

My hands,
not my stamina,
reveal my age—
leopard-spotted,
elephant-skin-wrinkled
from many days of
beach and garden sun.
On the right, two fingers
start to curl inward,
like my father's did.

They may display their years,
but I hold precious these appendages.
For hours at a time
they command a volleyball,
write stories and poems,
are an instrument for
the intention of healing.
My hands are strong and capable,
valued as they are—
marked, lined
with graceful deformity.

## Late Bloomer

I didn't write my first poem
at five or sit in trees reading
Dickinson's lines at fifteen.
None of that came for a long time.
Not in my twenties, thirties, or even forties.

At fifty-seven I wrote my first real poem.
Now they float to the surface with
the dawning of the day or
sometimes a full moon will light
their way into being.

# At Last

At last, a tuning in
to my own season.

A time for contemplation
of my life's meaning.

A time for soul-searching
and stretching for authentic being.

A time for introspection
and choosing new paths.

A time for compassion,
an awareness of the greater needs.

And also, a time for love and openness,
a full-throated tenderness for all.

# Window Shopping for Words

I love to go window shopping
for words. My fingers walk
from site to site seeing them
displayed in all their finery.

I imagine what the lines of my poem
would look like in each ensemble.
Is it the perfect little black dress of a word?
I try each one on for size. Does it
fit me and my feelings? Is it a vintage find
that I can redo or remake? Is it a magical
word that resonates with my style or one that
makes my poem look lumpy and lifeless?

Sometimes I grab the word, get home
and find it's just not right, not the real me;
it's too trendy or the satin doesn't swish
like I had hoped it would. Then I need to
return it and begin again.

# Homage to my Single-Mindedness

My mind rarely allows me to give in,
or give up; persistently, it whispers
close to my ear, *There is always a way.*

It keeps me awake at all hours
until it discovers the missing piece
to whatever puzzle is puzzling me.

It applauds as I struggle to
learn computer skills
and repair the vacuum cleaner,
an ice maker, my iPhone, the dishwasher.

My mind is dogged like a cat
patiently waiting for its prey,
encouraging as a grandmother who proudly
claims there is little I cannot accomplish,
obstinate as a child who declares
*I can do it by myself!*

My mind's single-mindedness
has made me confident, determined,
certain there is next to nothing I cannot do.

# Meaning of Christmas

Christmas doesn't call to me;
    I've even been accused of being a scrooge.
Although I love the original story—
    a child born to humble beginnings
becoming history's greatest healer
    and teacher of love and kindness.

A Christmas miracle, on the
    other hand, has my full attention.
We were given one once
    when our son was born too early.
We pray for another now;
    my belief in possibility is pure.

# Those Who Tend the Fire

— after a line by Birch Dwyer

*Your falling apart magnificence,*
say the grandmothers who tend the fire
just for me, *is what we love most
about you.*

*You were never meant to know it all,
be it all, achieve it all, possess it all,
you were only meant to be
the beautiful being that is you.*

They are dressed in long skirts,
as I have always pictured them,
surrounding me with a yearning
for their child come home.

They tease not to take life
so seriously, insist that loss is
merely an illusion for my learning.
The women say they have also seen the joy
I embody from each and every day.

*She's the one,* they whisper,
*the one who holds our love in her heart,
carries it forward into the future—
the one who accepted our gifts.*

*This I Believe*

# A Time my Own

Birdsong awakens me to first light
    through bamboo slats;
    consciousness drifts forward.

The things to do are many,
    but life has taught me
    to honor morning stillness.

Respiration slows and deepens,
    becomes more aware,
    bathing the space around my heart.

Tingles of energy flow
    on the breath, yielding
    trust, balance, and wonder.

The gift of sacred contemplation
    calmly centers, smooths
    rough edges from the day to come,
    like pieces of glass lovingly
        tumbled by the sea.

# My Voice

On the sacred wave of my voice
a story erupts from my heart.
It is a tale of unity, of relation, of love.

It encompasses every individual,
creature, and the natural world,
all equally of value,
all an original gift from the One.

The responsibility of my voice
is to weave the words together to
form a reminder of our blessedness,
our reasons for being,
all the oceans we embody expressing the light.

# Gratitude

Sacred Presence, receive
heartfelt gratitude for
feet on the earth
and the euphoria this brings;

the journey of love
in all its eclectic forms;

prolific health, strength,
and energy oftentimes reserved
for the young;

a clear faith in integral goodness;

appreciation for the undulating beauty of our world—
eyes to perceive and legs to roam;

an open heart to sense Spirit's spark
in another's eyes;

peacefulness that has become
a default setting;

the manna of a divine purpose—
my swirling lodestar,
the wonder and miracle of
healing vibration and light;

the solace of quiet mornings
lulled by joyful contemplation;

the muse who gifts me
inspiration and creativity;

angels who hold my hands,
whisper softly, point out a path,
and keep me out of harm's way.

## Go Easy

Go easy, my soul
    through days
that threaten your heart
    and guide you to your knees
spent and humble,
    as well as days of glorious
lightness of being, when weightless
    you are uplifted as if on wings.

Moreover, the many days of
    breaths and sighs wherein
sorrow and joy lie side by side
    tenderly clasping hands
as the moments roll by
    like a moving picture,
remembering only at the end
    that it was just a dream.

# Imagine if

> — after *Ask and It Is Given*,
> Esther and Jerry Hicks

we were taught as children,
    in school and at home, that
    we are vibrational beings
    able to use natural laws
    to create the happiest of times.

we understood that
    we are extensions of infinite Source,
    here to have fun and create;
    whatever we give our attention to
    brings more of the same;
    we can tune into a place where
    everything is taken care of.

we were presented with this new way
    of thinking and this helped us
    to craft a spectacular life.

# The Path to Choose

— for Allen

When you find yourself
at a junction,
two paths
or more ahead,
and you know not which
to choose
to lead you
toward your greater good,
ask.
Sit in stillness
and ask.

The answer
that is true for you
will come,
often not
on your schedule.
Be patient.

While you wait,
use a trick
my son taught me.
In your mind's eye
picture each journey.
See and feel and experience
each direction.

And if you still
have no idea,
well then,
take the path more overgrown,
even though
or especially because
your heart beats quicker
as a result of it.

# Motherhood

A woman swimming through
    the open seas of motherhood
      is like a piece of clear glass
      with sharp edges
    evolving over time
through years of waves
and tides and being
    rubbed by the elements
      transforming slowly
      to smooth sea glass
    murky, points worn down
softer, easier to hold.

# Dear one, whenever you are able

try to be kind
and open,
play like a child,
smile and laugh
a lot,

contemplate the forest,
breathe in the scent of the sea,
be conscious of love in its many forms,

welcome suggestions
from beyond,
gently release your fears
and the desire to control
the ebb and flow,

feel life in its totality,
accept all paths traveled,
forgive hurts held on to,

allow your energy to uplift,
be thankful for blessings received,

remember the remarkable
being and body of light
that you are.

# Questions to Myself

— for Elena

Can you hold close to your bosom
the knowing that all will change?

With this understanding, do you have the courage
and the faith to walk out into each new day?

What choice do you have?
You have borne the agony and the joy of impermanence.

The response is clear—
to face your life with either fear or allowing.
Open your hands; let life flow through them.

The primal urge to grasp is futile,
like attempting to contain water in a sieve.
It will not give you what you want or need.

Feel the coming and the going;
be exhilarated in the both.
Delight in the dance
of each precious present moment,
float with the tides as they rise and fall,
lovingly held upon the waves of time.

# Thank you

for the gift of life
the blessing of family
a constant cocoon of faith
the sanctuary of home
whispers of intuition
unexpected grace
the tenderness of a guiding hand
the soothing energy of Mother Earth
innate trust to remain open
the glorious feeling of creativity
love that knows no limits
connection with all, to all
the treasure of days strung like pearls
    on a strand bequeathed to me.

# This I Believe

I believe that goodness
is the root and core of all of life;

an act of kindness
is the best reaction to any action;

there is no separation between me
and my fellow living beings;

a benevolent river of consciousness exists
that holds us forever afloat in our experience;

each time we respond to an encounter
it is from a choice of fear or love;

we live to the best of our ability,
receive and give in our own capacity;

with love, trust, and allowing
everything can be sorted out.

I believe in openness, in being vulnerable,
and in making a practice of our shared breath.

# Water

*I would love to live*
*Like a river flows*
*Carried by the surprise*
*Of its own unfolding.*
                    John O'Donohue, "Fluent"

When life gets stuck in eddies
and ebb is felt more than flow,
I return to memories of water.

Gently rocked in rhythmic waves,
I stroke
onward into depths unknown.

Water always soothes me,
bestows peace of heart and mind,
along with answers from a bottomless beyond.

## Reiki is

calming, opening,
magical, miraculous,
always accessible,
healing, a helping hand
in times of trouble,
flowing, circulating currents,
truth and transformation,
all-encompassing,
clearing for life's stuck spots,
a sister and brotherhood
of caring support,
a warm cozy blanket
to keep fears at bay,
love in all its splendor.

## Equanimity

I like this word,
not how it sounds, especially;
it's impossible to pronounce,
for me at least,
and my spelling of it
never comes out right.

The meaning is what grabs me,
holds me spellbound—
just the thought that it's possible
not to judge experiences
as good or bad,
joyful or causing pain.

Once, I searched my brain
for days trying to remember
this term, wanting to put it to use,
but it had been temporarily erased
from my mind's hard drive.

When it showed its face on a page,
I was delighted to encounter the forgotten word;
of course, this occurred after
reaching an equanimous state
regarding whether I ever found it again.

## Los Angeles

— for Guillermina

I met a woman who sees angels.
At Christmas she says
    the gates of heaven open a sliver more
    and millions of angels swirl out,
    flying down a funnel of radiance,
    rippling to earth,
    bestowing spheres of light, *esferas de luz,*
    gifts from the Divine.

They land on every home; each corner
    is graced with the luminous gift
    of love and joy.

        \*

A special prayer bequeathed to my friend
    by her grandmother, *abuelita a nieta—*

*Ángel de mi guarda, mi dulce compañía,*
    *no me dejes solo, ni de noche ni de día,*
    *que, sin ti, me perdería.*

Guardian angel, my sweet companion,
    do not leave my side, not in nighttime nor in day,
    for without you, I would lose my way.

        \*

My keepers are close, *siempre;*
    petitions for anyone, everyone,
    I sense they are heeded.

## Chosen

I believe we are all chosen
to be channels for creation,
and responding to this calling
with openness can lead to great joy.

I was a channel for my son and daughter
to come through, a purpose that has given me
the most perpetual happiness.

I am a channel for writing, the flow coming
in the form of stories and poems,
and I sense the guiding hand
that midwives the words through me.

I am a channel for energy whenever
I give, receive, or teach Reiki;
that opening has led to unimaginable gifts,
and a raft to hold on to when
it seems my world is sinking.

We are each given endless opportunities
to be channels; some appear small,
others, like those above,
inconceivably alter our lives.

The one thing they have in common
is an opening to love.

# The Puzzle

— for Tyann, my first Reiki teacher

My teacher believes
we are each
a piece of the puzzle.

Alone, we cannot
resolve the chaos
erupting on this planet.

Yet we can
unearth and foster
our rare true gifts
to satisfy our share
of what is vital
for this world to become
a kinder, more loving
home to live in.

# Thanksgiving

> — dedicated to my mother
> on Thanksgiving Day

It feels right to be thankful
for the grace of gifts given
and received.

Forevermore, the velvet
soothing of love.
Existence in its entirety
craving to be known.

Breath and sighs, the wonder
of a complying body.
An essential spark
that eternally nudges,
gently impels,
in a labyrinth
towards communion.

Trust in wholeheartedly allowing
an uncharted course.
Thank you, I sense
your innate presence.
It sustains me, always.

# Compassion

Compassion dresses in soft clothes,
a bright paisley print shawl
draped over her shoulders,
comfy shoes, for all the distances
she hopes to cover.  She has the look
of someone's grandmother or
Mother Earth herself.

Compassion cocks her head,
beckons, then reaches out
her hand to you with a smile.
She loves to think of things
to make you happy,
to help you live your life
like a love song.

Some aspire to return
her benevolence in kind,
and that could be okay,
but Compassion says
it warms her heart
when kindness is paid forward.

Compassion transforms fear to grace,
disease to healing, hate to love.
She gently whispers,
*Give to me your discomfort
and let's make of it a rainbow.*

# Things I Didn't Understand Were God

The light at any time of day,
especially when morning sun first rises
above an eastern hill, I didn't understand
was God illuminating the way.

Birds crying out on high
in a bright blue heaven, blissful in
their gift of flight, I couldn't understand
was God singing out our names.

Enthusiastic smiles on children's faces,
their elation at being able to create,
I came to understand were exclamation
marks on God's rounds of applause.

Trees dropping leaves and the magic
of an unfailing rebirth, I soon
understood was God's prompting us
to savor the circle of life.

Liquid warmth of compassion
coursing from heart through hands,
now I understand is the most glorious
of all God's graces.

## A New Day

*Nothing is worth more than this day.*
             — Johann Wolfgang von Goethe

Each morning a brand new
blank slate to write on—
　　a dawn of limitless possibilities
　　　　to fill this passel of hours
　　to see the surrounding beauty and connect
　　　　on a soul level with the people on your path
　　to catch that flicker of recognition
　　　　in their eyes.

Open your heart to whispers
from an inner wellspring
　　put yourself in another's shoes
　　try to ease the needs you see craving to be filled.

Breathe out love like it's your last day—
　　the often-unrecalled secret to a
　　rose-colored life, a practice worth perfecting.

You only need to see random crosses
　　along roadside edges to remember that not all
　　are graced with one more clean page.

## That Ultimate Date

— for Teresa

After we received the news,
I lay awake in the soft quiet
of night thinking—
the days of our living
are bookended
by two points in time,
one of our birth,
the other of our death.

That ultimate date hovers
over our head, connected
by a thread so thin
we forget it is there,
like a child falling asleep
after hours of play
forgets a weightless balloon
tied to her wrist.

# Another Approach

No matter how carefully we reside in this world,
    hard times come.  Understanding this,
    do we choose to live hunched over,
    in fear of hypothetical threat
    around every looming corner?

Or do we attempt another approach,
    a more trusting, unguarded stance—
    shoulders back, chest open,
    laughing and extending love to the
    certainty of an uncertain experience?

# A Binding Thread

This home in which I live
is the warp and the weave
of creation.

We are woven from light,
shaped by magic,
from brightly colored strands.

We can elect to be a
filament of unity, connecting ourselves
with our true natures.

It is a choosing;
I believe that offering to be
a binding thread in the tapestry
leads to more magic,
much, much more.

# Graduation

Picture a vibrant graduation party,
one with multi-colored balloons,
friends and family are dancing
merrily to tantalizing beats,
celebration is in the air,
a poet reads her poem lovingly penned
for future good wishes,
caps are thrown into the air.

What if this were a celebration of death?
A much-anticipated commencement
to be applauded, after years
of lessons, questions asked and answered.
Not tears of sadness, only joy
to float our loved ones forward
into the next field of living,
balloons untethered, set free into the sky.

# When My Time Here

When my time here
is coming to a close,
I want to look back
with satisfaction and
affection on a life well-lived.

No regrets for
things not tried out of fear.
No regrets for
not enough love offered.
No regrets for
not appreciating the beauty
of our world to the fullest
and the perfectness of
how the puzzle fits together.

*World Wound Down*

# A Vision of Healing

I float on a gentle sea,
legs and arms spread like a starfish,
lulled by waves that gently rock me.

As I gaze up to benevolent clouds,
a radiant beam lowers into my awaiting heart,
accompanied by the sound of angelic chimes.

It fills me with love, peace,
and perfect being, my body a vessel
for the delivery of loving care to the world.

Warm brilliance blazes from my center,
out palms, feet, root, and crown, streaming
over sea and land, alighting on all in its wake.

On the opposite side of the globe, energy merges
like ocean waves, sprays out into a light-filled
mist, sprinkling down on every fragment
of our beloved earth and extended family.

All are loved.  All are offered healing.
All are held in infinite hands.

*March 16, 2020*

# We Are Told

We are told to stay home;
if we need groceries or gas
    not to congregate;
to keep a social distance of
    at least six feet;
to wash our hands repeatedly;
as of yesterday
    we are on lockdown,
    although the rules for that
    are not clear.

We are told
this is a pandemic of
    hazardous proportions;
it is possible to carry the virus
    and not know you have it;
that thousands have died
    in China, Italy, Iran, and Spain;
in last night's news—
    fifty percent of Californians
    could become infected.

        So, I turn off the broadcast,
        hold my dear cat,
        feel his purring vibration calm me;
        I take walks near our country home,
        thankful for my life
        and our family being together.

        And I remember that
        everything heals in one way or another.
        And this too will pass.

*March 20, 2020*

## Sheltered at Home

Home is a cocoon for my precious tribe,
content now with this unknown number
of days in each other's company.

We cook mainly comfort food
with treats of homemade cookies and popcorn,
share in conversation and laughter, take walks,
choose movies to watch, games to play.

I like how the calendar looks with blank squares
and how it feels to live that freedom,
reveling in the solitude and seclusion
from external distractions, as we each do
our separate jobs under a shared roof,
but in different rooms.

Nights are deep with hours of sleep,
countless dreams that disappear
with the light; I let my hair
hang loose as it dries,
no makeup—only yoga pants, socks,
and long-sleeved tees.

I wonder how we will look back
on these days, what we will learn
and then change in our doing.

*March 27, 2020*

## Animals During the Pandemic

Do the animals sense how
we've changed the way we live?

A doe and fawn lie on our hill,
watching us inside at the table, their ears
like radar dishes, alert, in case someone
enters the driveway. But no one does.

A ring-necked snake sidewinds in
S curves, stops to scrunch his coral red
tail into a tight curl, striving to flee from
the threat of our inquisitive shadows.

A hawk flies low overhead,
then perches in the sycamore,
seemingly to commune; she must
have ancient wisdom to share.

What we can learn from the animals to apply now—
    perseverance;
    living the moment as it exists;
    concentrating on instinctual tasks like feeding our
        young, our old, ourselves;
    keeping loved ones safe;
    contending with whatever the land, the sky
        and mankind bring.

*March 27, 2020*

## A Friend

As I walk up the hill
after wheeling trash cans
down to the road, a giant
winged shadow passes over.

I call out and he circles
around on windy currents,
once, twice, three times,
curious to see who has beckoned.

Even a vulture can be a friend,
in this time of isolation.

*April 2, 2020*

# Land of the Free

Over the land of the free
And the home of the brave
For a time, liberties have been sacrificed
In favor of a greater common welfare.

That the star-spangled banner
Long may continue to wave,
We as a people do stand united,
And lend a caring hand to one another.

This our beloved motto be:
In God we trust forevermore,
Faith in better days yet to come,
A nation blessed and peace restored.

*April 4, 2020*

# The Significance of Corona

I ask my younger brother,
fountain of information,
why the virus is called *corona*
or crown in English.

He explains the name comes
from its shape under a microscope.
Interesting, I think.
A message, maybe.

Crown chakra,
at the top of our heads,
a connecting link between us
and Source.

Is the pandemic
a not-so-gentle nudge
to wake us up
to what is truly needed?


April 5, 2020

## 20/20 Vision

When it came time to choose
resolutions for a new decade,
I thought long and hard,
decided rather to ask for 20/20 vision
for myself and the rest of humanity
going forward, expressly for the
year of that same number.

Who would have known,
a few months ago,
that a trouble would arise
asking us to retreat from
our everyday, busy lives—
forcing us to slow down, providing time
to contemplate a clearer sight for our future.

*April 12, 2020*

## Giving Up Routines

My husband gave up
daily lunches with co-workers,
Friday or Saturday date nights out with me
for pasta and a shared glass of wine.

He gave up afternoons at the gym—
his workout, sauna, and hot water spa,
and relaxing beers with his long-time friend
at a local brewing company.

His need for routine is greater than mine.

Because he is possibly compromised health-wise,
we plan for days' worth of meals, fewer grocery
trips to reduce risks of contagion,

we not knowing until four weeks in,
he had refused to part with his morning,
made-to-order green drink,
remained a devoted customer at the juice bar
each day, while the rest of us were
fervently attempting to protect him.

*April 12, 2020*

# Good News

First hot spring day on our California coast,
cows and horses feasting on green hills,
a jackrabbit runs lickety-split across a field,
his loping stride, stride, stride,
and then an airborne bound,
how good that flight must feel.

The news last night reports
as of Easter Sunday we are over the hump;
new cases of the dreaded virus
diminishing instead of escalating.

Our circle of women, each sequestered
in her own home, a few hours earlier
had sent intentions remotely,
for a healing world.

Hallelujah!

*April 14, 2020*

## Before the pandemic

bedazzled by gypsies of diversion,
distraction was a full-force way of living—

go out for a movie or concert, Thai or Italian,
coffee or ice cream, a drink with a friend,
travel here or there, work till we drop,
attend endless meetings and classes,
pick up laundry and library books, shop—

any number of addictions to pleasure,
to the detriment of family togetherness
and time in silence.

Lockdown—a sudden and total stop
to outside entertainments, entreated to
stay home, sequestered with housemates
and ourselves.

Not easy. But there may be shifts
in thinking to embrace, priorities to rearrange,
a loosening of the constant striving
for more.

If we open our eyes a little wider,
a clearer sight is within our view,
more easily pictured since
an act of nature quieted the outer noise.

April 29, 2020

## Pandemic Pandemonium

*Don't it always seem to go*
*that you don't know what you've got*
*till it's gone.*
             Joni Mitchell, "Big Yellow Taxi"

The world has wound down,
like scenes from a poorly
rehearsed sci-fi production;
an add-on to the plot
even includes the Pentagon's
confirming the existence of UFOs.

At a snap of the fingers, so much changed.
People sick, people scared, people dying.
Businesses closed: stores, offices, theaters,
parks, gyms, trails, beaches.

Plans canceled: school activities, surgeries, sports,
meetings, celebrations, memorials.
What can be managed in the virtual
realm moves to Zoom.

People sick, people scared, people dying.
Everyone wears a mask now,
eyes obscured with unease,
silently measuring a six-foot
bubble of supposed safety.

Protests to lift lockdown occur alongside
protests to continue isolation,
political parties blame and bicker.
We were blindsided, innocent to how quickly
what had been built up could crumble down.

People sick, people scared, people dying—
pandemic pandemonium.
America the strong,
one nation under God,
a not-so-distant memory.

*May 5, 2020*

## Lockdown Lifted

I feel weighted down,
heavy of limb and heart,
like when the ocean current
sucks at my legs,
keeping me from the shore.

We are told we can go out
again, be with others,
but still masked and distant.
I am not afraid, just used to the comfort
and confines of my cocoon.

How to bridge the chasm between
the old and the altered worlds?
Nothing beckons me
from the outside;
everything I need is here.

*June 7, 2020*

## Sentinels

How the trees have grown
around us,
with a surplus of winter
and spring rains.

The sycamore we planted
as a sapling soars three stories high.
The oaks facing the house
have morphed into
one tree with two trunks.

A grove of eucalyptus,
their silver sifting leaves
testing the waters of the sky,
confirm life will continue
to march on.

The trees form a sacred den,
shelter us from external
elemental ravages.
Sentinels of sentient existence,
wise keepers cradling
my spirit in their limbs.

*June 7, 2020*

## Roadside Litter

Years ago, I'd leave the house
    each morning at seven
and meet my friends
    to hike our hillside trails.

On Wednesdays, the day
    the trash truck came,
I would take a plastic bag
    to pick up litter along the way.

Those habits are lost to time;
    this morning I go alone.
At nine, eased by sleep and dreams,
    I leave to walk our country roads.

Strangely, the shoulders are nearly devoid of debris:
    a few wrappers, a water bottle, a can.
What shocks me most—two paper face masks,
    blown probably from car dashboards,
one fading on a barbed wire fence,
    another on the ground among weeds.

It has been four months of spreading virus.
    How innocent we were a year ago.
    How much we took for granted.

*July 11, 2020*

# A Continuance of Change

A strife-free life does not exist
      but in longing, like parching thirst
      brings dreams of verdant streams.

It is a world forever broken open
      by a continuance of change,
      the disruption of ordered things.

How not to lose heart?
Where are the guiding signs?
Can faith be enough?

Faint whisperings float by my ear,
*Accept what is, love the world no matter what.*

      Acceptance, the drumbeat that will lead me home.

*July 15, 2020*

# The Mask

Breathing is hindered behind a mask,
requires a bit of attentiveness,
and I realize belatedly that people
cannot see me smiling at them;
communicating compassion with
my eyes takes some practice.

I guess my mask is comfortable:
cotton, black with a golden print.
I take shallow breaths and yearn
for days when it was not a necessity.

In line at the bank, seven or so people,
all masked and separated;
it's like I'm watching a scary movie,
hard to imagine this reality is ours.

*July 21, 2020*

# These Days

These days, I swim carefully
through my hours while I wait.

I lack the motivation to do much more,
only what is most necessary,
which means I have time to write
and sit in silence listening.

The rest: windows needing washing,
a cluttered desk of papers,
a house to clean, my list waiting to be ticked off—
all this for another time.
There's always tomorrow.
Or is there?

In motionless doldrums my ship drifts,
no wind fills my sails;
but somewhere buried leagues below,
like a treasure waiting to be found,
    is hope.

*July 22, 2020*

## Una Sacudida

I want someone to explain to me
what's up with this year;
a lot of crazy stuff is going on—
a global pandemic, protests,
antagonistic politics. California on fire,
front page news two days ago—
our county had the worst air quality
in the world.

We have lost family members
in May, July, and August.
Today the nuclear plant siren
pierced our hills and I thought, what now?
This one… thankfully… only a test.

There is a word in Spanish
that comes to mind—
*una sacudida*—a shaking up:
like a tremor so strong it is felt
hundreds of miles from its origin,
or a jolt of electricity from a finger
touching a bad socket.

This year feels like that;
it seems as if something—
Mother Earth? the universe? God?
wants our attention…
and is going to get it,
come hell or high water.

*August 22, 2020*

# The Grandmothers Answer

The children ask, how can we weather
this season of transformation,
    and the grandmothers answer:

Trust in your beautiful heart;
    be still and open to its presence.
Bow to your heart;
    place your healing hands upon it.

Give thanks for how far your heart has carried you;
    let it know you are prepared to learn.
Ask your heart
    to be your sacred mother.

The heart is wise.
The heart will speak.
    You need only pay close attention and love,
    to become a catalyst of light for the world.

*August 23, 2020*

## Practicing

Even after forty-plus years
of devoted practice,
when times get tough
I sometimes have trouble keeping
the faith that *this too shall pass.*

Today I try sitting in silence;
listing things I am thankful for;
listening to music that uplifts me;
writing a poem (this one);
holding my cat (on my lap now);
eating chocolate (the bar beside me is half eaten).

But in the end—
the virus is yet spreading;
the wildfires keep burning;
we are still living a prognosis
of impermanence.

*September 10, 2020*

# Questions Google Can't Answer

With technology mind-blowingly smart,
why can't a cure for cancer be found?

Can our planet possibly endure the damage
that's been done to it?

Will there ever be a time in the future
when war is not waged?

Is it realistic to believe there could be enough
respect between politicians and parties
so they could work together for the good of us all?

When will our beautiful, robin's-egg sky return,
the air not sooty with ash?

Will a time come when we can stop covering our faces
with masks, start hugging again?

What I *can* find easily on Google are the definitions
for doomsday, apocalypse, Armageddon.

In the kitchen, I inhale with my nose close
to freshly ground coffee and
the bluest of birds zings like an arrow
into a bush.

My cat meows his unwavering good morning,
never questioning our wonderful life.

*September 11, 2020*

# World Upside Down

The world
wound down,
quieted its
incessant sounds,
turned ways of living
all around,
hoped for new answers
to be found.
For now: topsy-turvy,
life upside down.

*September 17, 2020*

# A Recipe

I want to create a recipe for this time,
ingredients to be combined
to make a perfect batch of love
that we can feed all of humanity.

I might begin with compassion,
add cinnamon sticks for comfort,
mint to cool the rage hitting
the roof of heaven.

Acorn squash and pumpkin pieces
for sustenance, basil and curry—
anything I can think of
that might be a remedy for fear.

And carrots for courage,
to help us see the illusion
of separation, a big dash of patience,
along with cups and cups of hope.

*October 28, 2020*

# Because

*Finally I saw that worrying had come to nothing. And gave it up.*
*And took my old body and went out into the morning and sang.*
       Mary Oliver, "I Worried"

*What will happen to us today is completely unknown…*
*Whatever happens, our commitment is to use it to awaken*
   *our heart…*
*All activities should be done with one intention.*
*That intention is to realize our connection with all beings.*
       Pema Chödrön, The Places That Scare You

Because we love so deeply
but will never have enough days,
each morning, I want to remember
that the hours before me are a gift.

Let me push aside the unknown
like days-old, dried bread,
selecting instead a simple breakfast
of fruit and nourishing sunshine.

The birds sing open-heartedly
no matter who our next president might be,
even in a smoke-filled sky, and during
a pandemic that just won't go away.

2020, our year of great uncertainty—
personally, nationally, and globally;
it's an invitation, possibly, to choose.

The only reasonable plan I can see:
to sow love and kindness, instead of fear.

*November 6, 2020*

# Trespassing

> — after reading "At the Border" by
> Rosemerry Wahtola Trommer

When I set off from our home
for an afternoon walk
I had a destination in mind—
up to the end of our country road.
But when I arrived, feeling energized,
I took a left and continued on,
finally arriving at the gate
to an old utility road,
a place I used to walk almost daily.

*No Trespassing* signs are now posted,
reminding me of a poem I read this week
about a woman coming across
a forgotten sign she had put up eons before.
She no longer wished to keep people at bay,
so, she took it down.

\*

Hoping this could also be true
of whoever nailed these notices up
and already feeling a bit like an outlaw
every time I go out in public—
our state a few days ago returning to
shutdown for a second time this year,
even an alert blasting across our cell phones,
warning us to stay at home
except for the essential.

My thoughts being so,
I chose to steal behind the gate
and up the hill of silty sand-colored dirt,
past weathered ageless oaks,
eucalyptus trees touching thin clouds,
backlit lime green leaves of the manzanitas,
trunks a burnished carnelian,
then dried pampas grass stalks cackling
in the wind, the tops of pines tattling.

*

On the winding trails I lost my way,
couldn't find a path down to the distant road,
and my thoughts crept to the mountain lion
seen lounging in a tree, lazily gazing
at my friend's horse in its corral,
on this same hillside just last year.

*December 12, 2020*

# Month Ten

Stores still have lines outside,
and when I walk the aisles,
people rarely lift their eyes to mine,
concentrating on getting what is needed,
not crossing an imaginary line.

Our son, who contracted COVID at work
before Thanksgiving, flies home
from New York today, recovered thankfully.
During the holidays, our daughter works from here
for a company three thousand miles away;
twice within a month exposed to the virus,
she awaits results from the second test.
As I write a new hope rises, health workers
beginning to be inoculated with a vaccine.

Mostly, I keep fear at bay, and when unwanted
tremors raise their scary bogeyman faces,
I remind myself there is little I can control.
Meanwhile, I mainly stay home,
wear a mask and wash my hands.

Some anxiety must lie buried in a subconscious
cubbyhole; lately in my peopled dreams
I feel concern when we get too close,
which makes me wonder how long
we will continue to keep our distance.

*December 18, 2020*

My sincere gratitude goes to Cuesta College and its Emeritus program. In the fall of 2016, I entered a Composing Your Life Stories class taught by Russell Swanagon. I had never read or written poetry, but he believed some of my stories could be crafted into poems. He gave me ideas about how to do this and then pointed me to the works of Mary Oliver, the first complete books of poetry I read. I will be forever thankful to Russell for his guidance, which led to a major life shift toward writing. Thank you, also, to Sara Roahen, who later took over this class—for her creative weekly lessons and superb editing assistance on articles for publication and on this collection of poems. Also, thanks to my fellow writers who, over ten semesters, have written and read their stories openly and listened to mine.

Thank you to the Literary Nest for my first virtual poetry workshop, during which I started learning the tools of the trade. This and John Fox's Year of Poetic Medicine helped me garner the courage to present my work online. John's "The Sacredness of Trees" was the first workshop I attended in person. Thank you to Arts Obispo for my first opportunity to read a poem to a hall full of people, and for inviting me to participate in its ekphrastic poetry events held in conjunction with local galleries. To our Morro Bay/Los Osos poetry group, members of which graciously opened their arms to me several years ago—our continuing monthly sessions have taught me much about revision.

Special thanks to my friend, Blaire Kilbey, for offering her lovely painting for the cover. I am grateful for my friend Lonna Crane—fellow poet and Reiki Master, who has a larger collection of poetry books than our library does, and who generously lends them to me; and for my friend Nancy Ruiz, who has helped me edit pieces written in Spanish. To my friends John and Meiyun Chyan, and their vision many years ago that I would publish a book someday, I'm sorry I laughed. To all the rest of my family and friends who patiently read the poems I shared, thank you for being so supportive. And I'd be remiss not to be thankful for our cat, Roo, who sat on my lap day after day while I read and wrote poetry, and often participated in our Zoom sessions.

I have immense gratitude for the County of San Luis Obispo Public Libraries, where I have been an avid patron for more than fifty years— especially my first library in Shell Beach and later our community library in Arroyo Grande. During the pandemic they allowed me to order books of poetry through their Zip Books program. Being sheltered at home this year was made easier by the following: having these library books to read; Poets House 10-10-10 workshops; workshops facilitated by Birch Dwyer of Portland Women Writers; and a small Santa Barbara poetry group led by Perie Longo. Thank you, Perie, for your editing ideas on some of the poems in this collection. I want to also thank Ben Lawless of Penciled In for his creative book designing.

Thank you, to all seven of my Reiki teachers. In a synchronistic way, my first Reiki and writing classes started within a few days of each other, and I understand now that each of these practices inspires the other. It really has been a wonderful journey, and I thank every one of you from my heart.

www.ingramcontent.com/pod-product-compliance
Lightning Source LLC
Chambersburg PA
CBHW060158050426
42446CB00013B/2896